D1144047

GLOBAL INDUSTRIES
UNCOVERED

THE FASHION INDUSTRY

ROSIE WILSON

WAYLAND

Published in 2012 by Wayland

Copyright © Wayland 2012

Wayland
338 Euston Road
London NW1 3BH

Wayland Australia
Level 17/207 Kent Street
Sydney NSW 2000

Series Editor: Claire Shanahan
Editor: Susie Brooks
Consultant: Steph Warren
Designer: Rebecca Painter
Picture Researcher: Shelley Noronha

British Library Cataloguing in Publication Data
Wilson, Rosie.
   The fashion industry. -- (Global industries
        uncovered)
   1. Fashion design--Juvenile literature.
   2. Fashion merchandising--Juvenile literature.
   3. Clothing trade--Juvenile literature.
   4. Industrial location--Juvenile literature.
   5. Globalization--Economic aspects--Juvenile
   literature.
   I. Title II. Series
   338.4'7687-dc22

ISBN 978 0 7502 6945 2

Picture acknowledgements
6, 8, 9, 10, 15, 17, 18, 19, 27 EASI-Images/Rob
Bowden; 13, 20, 32, 34, 36 Getty Images; 21 ©
KIN HEUNG/Reuters/Corbis; 22 credit: Topfoto;
28 © Frank Miller/Corbis; 30 EASI-Images/Roy
Maconachie; 33 © WWD/Condé Nast/Corbis; 35
© MIKE CASSESE/ Reuters/ Corbis; 38 Joerg
Boethling/Alamy; 40 People Tree

Printed in China

Wayland is a division of Hachette Children's
Books, an Hachette UK company.
www.hachette.co.uk

Contents

CASE STUDIES UNCOVERED

The world is our wardrobe!

Emily gets into her new clothes ready for school. Today is a non-uniform day, but she needs her sports kit too. She'll wear trainers anyway – the newest design, which cost five times as much as the rest of her outfit. Her t-shirt was a bargain from the store nearby and it looks just like one worn by a celebrity in Emily's favourite magazine. Emily never looks at labels on the inside, but if she did, she would find that the t-shirt came from the Dominican Republic, the jeans from Tunisia and the trainers from China. Her jewellery – another bargain – was made in India. None of the workers who made Emily's clothes were paid enough to live, but she doesn't know this.

Young people enjoy shopping in Harajuku, a district of Tokyo, Japan. Fashion styles vary widely, even within a single street.

Going global

Global industries work across nations and continents, producing and selling in several countries, and affecting the lives of people around the world. The fashion industry involves everyone who makes, sources or sells products (clothes, accessories, coats and shoes) for customers to wear. It also includes the producers of raw materials such as cotton, metals, rubber and wool. Sometimes the clothing industry is called the garment or apparel industry. The global fashion industry has several centres of production, where clothes are made, and other centres of retail, where they are sold.

Globalisation: a shrinking world

Globalisation means that we live in a smaller, more connected, more interdependent world. Physically, the world is not smaller, but it feels smaller because we have access to more of it. Geographical distances seem nearer because it takes less time now to travel to them or communicate between them. This has been made possible by improvements in technology. Mobile phones, the internet, low-cost flights and cheaper cars are all examples of this. Global connections are faster, easier and cheaper, which means that industries use them more. It can be easy for those living in more developed countries (MDCs) to take this for granted, but the technological revolution has not taken place at the same rate all over the world. As a result, some countries have benefited more than others from globalisation.

Winners and losers

The global fashion industry has both winners and losers. Powerful global companies make large profits and provide their customers in MDCs with a wide range of products at low prices. Less developed countries (LDCs) such as China, Turkey and Bangladesh provide labour and benefit from the industry, with new roads, schools and hospitals being built.

However, many individuals in LDCs work long hours in factories making fashion products, and do not earn a living wage (enough money daily to feed their family and provide shelter). Poverty levels remain high in these places, while many people in the UK, the USA and Japan, for example, have more than they need and can afford to buy a new fashion item every week. There are losers in MDCs too, as fashion companies buy from factories and contractors all across the world, so local manufacturers have closed down due to competition.

> *I am angry because of what is happening to these workers, who sew the clothes we wear... We need to expose the corporations that are growing ever richer off the backs of workers trapped in appalling conditions in the developing world.*

Anita Roddick, *The Economist*, July/August 2004

A fashion world

Fashion is a global industry because it affects everyone in the world. Clothing is a basic need to keep us warm and protect our bodies, but today clothing also sends messages about what kind of person the wearer is. Billions of pounds are involved in making, transporting and selling clothing, accessories and shoes. Some people spend much of their income on 'high fashion' items, trendy because they were bought extremely recently. Each year the UK consumes over 2 million tonnes of clothing and textiles, at a value of more than £38 billion. Many people worldwide are involved in this process at different stages. After first use, the things we wear often start another journey – to charity shops, bins, or sometimes to be resold far across the globe.

Fashion connections

Fashion has a history of global connections and has played an important role in the rise of global trade and globalisation. The 'silk road' from India to Europe brought cloths and gems as early as the 4th century, but the route was difficult and dangerous. Ships exploring the oceans to find a faster, easier route discovered the American continent and Africa, and eventually circumnavigated the globe.

Cotton, too, has a global history, and the trade triangle (including cotton) that developed between Europe, North and South America and Africa fuelled the transatlantic slave trade (see page 24). The desire for precious stones and gold is present in many cultures, and such treasures have often been traded for other products or used as symbols of wealth, royalty and power.

Most fashion products travel many miles around the world before reaching the consumer. Many are transported in shipping containers like these.

Shoppers stroll around the Queen Victoria Building shopping centre in Sydney, Australia. The centre has over 200 shops, many of them selling global brands, and is also a popular place to eat, meet friends and relax.

SPOTLIGHT

Why has the global fashion industry grown?

Global trends

Trends and styles spread across the globe in various ways. They are publicised through the global media (films, magazines, etc), and through transnational companies (TNCs) who sell the same products in many countries. Patterns of employment have boosted spending too, as most people work in services (shops, offices, hospitals, schools, etc) in many countries. These types of job often require people to look smart, even attractive. It is not acceptable in some careers to be 'out-of-fashion'.

Shopping habits

The purpose of shopping has changed from buying basic essentials to being a leisure activity. Purchasing products has also become a sign of wealth and status — for example, a BMW or a Chanel shopping bag mean the same thing in Beijing, Nairobi, London and Rio. Consumption is part of our global culture now, and a way to relax or spend time with others. Shopping centres also provide leisure facilities such as cinemas and restaurants. However, during times of economic hardship there is usually a fall in consumption, causing problems for many fashion retailers, and raising questions about the future of the industry.

Technology

The technology and machinery that make fashion items enable global production to work. Factories can mass-produce, and transportation costs are low per item when quantities are high, so it is worth sourcing materials and labour from around the world. Fabric is woven and spun easily using large machines, and shoes can be mass-produced, too. Jewellery parts are often cast or moulded using machinery and powered tools, in contrast to the laborious hand-crafting of the past.

Fashion locations

Many countries in the world used to have their own garment industry. Now, different stages of the process are located in different places, including rural areas, industrial sites, distribution centres and retail stores (in cities and their surrounds). Globalisation has led to garments being made, finished and labelled in several different countries before reaching their final destination. Newly built shopping areas are the most popular, therefore city centres need to regularly change in order to attract consumers. Online shopping is becoming more widely used. Although market stalls are no longer a regular source for fashion items in MDCs, they still play a major role in LDCs, and discarded clothes are also exported to these markets to be resold.

Market sellers in Jinja, Uganda, arrange clothing to be sold. After first use, many fashion items are exported to second-hand markets in LDCs.

Rising economies

Fast-developing nations play their own part in shaping the fashion industry. For example, in India, due to a flourishing economy, some people have more money to spend on consumer goods including clothing and fashion accessories, shoes and watches. India was the 12th-richest nation in the world in 2007. However, although US$36 billion was spent in India on clothing and fashion accessories in 2007, around 80 per cent of the country's population live on US$2 a day or less. The majority, therefore, have little access to the fashion industry, highlighting the imbalance in wealth that is typical of many nations, especially those developing fast.

SPOTLIGHT

Export processing zones

Export processing zones (EPZs) are areas set up within a country to attract foreign investors, often to produce goods to be sold abroad. Fashion factories that locate themselves in an EPZ can benefit from the cheaper labour of that country and also from lower or no taxes. LDCs use these zones to develop industry and provide jobs, but there are many cases where labour laws and human rights have been violated in EPZ workplaces, and the laws surrounding these areas are often unclear. Sometimes these zones can be industry-specific — there is a jewellery zone in Thailand and a leather zone in Turkey, for example. In China there are several special economic zones, which are similar to EPZs.

Time for change?

Some experts say that consumers are becoming concerned about inequality in the fashion industry. Ethical clothing, accessories and footwear are now popular, and are even offered by some mainstream companies. Financial problems and rising living costs (including food and energy prices) affect shopping patterns. The cost of production may rise if energy becomes more expensive. If consumers become aware of the issues surrounding their products, they may demand that workers are paid a living wage, by influencing the law, or by choosing carefully where they shop. This too will make production cost more, and each fashion item will be slightly more expensive, as it has been in the past.

> *Customers want good value, but they care more than ever how food and clothing products are made.*
>
> Former M&S chief executive Stuart Rose, 2006

The production and retail of the fashion industry makes a small group of people richer, and keeps poverty levels high in some countries. Fashion workers suffer from exhaustion and ill-health, whereas consumers benefit from cheaper-than-ever prices.

Relocation, relocation, relocation

The relocation of production has created pockets of poverty around the world, where mills and factories have closed, causing job losses. Examples of this are textile mills in Northern England and garment factories in Toronto, Canada. Local production is better for the environment, as the clothes miles (the total miles an item is transported before being sold) are reduced, so less carbon dioxide is emitted into the atmosphere. However, because large-scale global production is cheaper, it now dominates the industry.

Controlling trade

Free trade is trade that happens between countries without quotas or tariffs on imports and exports, and without subsidies. The price paid depends on the forces of a free market economy (see below). The international trade system is not entirely free, as tariffs, quotas and subsidies control trade, especially between MDCs and LDCs. Some countries subsidise their cotton farmers by paying them yearly to continue to produce cotton. Rich countries use quotas to restrict the amount of foreign imports entering their country. This protects the industry in their own countries. The Multi-Fibre Arrangement (MFA) was a quota system that controlled imports of textiles and clothing into rich countries between 1974 and 2004. When it was lifted, China's strong and growing industry, previously restricted, dominated the fabric and wider fashion market, causing many other nations' industries to decline.

SPOTLIGHT

Free market economies

A free market economy is a trading situation where the price of goods or services is decided by consumer demand and global supply. For example, cotton and diamonds are both goods that are in high demand, but cotton is more readily available than diamonds are, which makes diamonds cost much more than cotton. Companies can influence the price of goods too, by controlling or restricting the supply. This helps them to make more profit.

How fame fuels demand

Celebrities and stars are extremely popular in many countries, and the glamorous global careers of women like Victoria Beckham, Sarah Jessica Parker and Scarlett Johansson play an important part in the fashion industry. Designers provide free clothes to certain women, who act as an advert for that product in magazines, on TV and when photographed in the streets. Because many women aspire to be like these stars, buying similar clothes is also very popular. Although *haute couture* (high fashion) clothing is too expensive for most people, an affordable version is usually mass-produced for the general public, so high street companies are also dependent on these celebrities to sell clothes for them. Factory contracts can be created simply based on a celebrity's chosen outfit, but these contracts have very short deadlines. This forces factory employees to work overtime in order to keep their jobs and meet the MDCs' demand for celebrity style.

Celebrity stars such as Victoria Beckham and Katie Holmes, pictured here at an Armani event, play an important role in the global fashion industry.

> *Women are...scouring the website to bag the latest celebrity trends. Shoppers can search [for clothes] by their favourite celebrity as well as by style. Its teen clientele can snap up a £38 lace dress inspired by one worn by actress Mischa Barton, or a £28 floral number à la Ms Hilton.*
>
> The Guardian, writing about Asos.com, a fashion website, 2008

Infrastructure

The global fashion industry, especially the export industry, has helped some countries in their development of infrastructure. Global trade routes need transportation, so there has been an improvement in roads and development of ports and airports to allow quick and efficient shipment of goods. The industry has contributed to urbanisation, as factories have been built on what was previously agricultural land. These factories need reliable electrical power, so the power infrastructure of some countries has developed. Power stations have been built, and rivers dammed to generate hydro-electric power. In the countries where garments and accessories are retailed, shopping areas play an important part in town and city planning. As shopping has increased, more retail space is needed for global brands.

Population

The global fashion industry impacts on patterns and trends in population, too. In Latin America and Asia, for example, many people migrate towards urban areas and business districts that have factories. Labour exploitation in many factories has a negative impact on the health and standard of living of whole communities. In some cases, child labour is still used. The populations of MDCs are affected by the fashion industry as well. For example, during the 1990s and first years of the 21st century, there has been a worrying obsession with dieting and other lifestyle choices, aimed at helping women to fit fashionable clothes and look similar to the models and celebrities who market them.

SPOTLIGHT

Bangladesh

The garment industry in Bangladesh is worth £11 billion, employs 3.5 million workers, and makes up almost 80 per cent of all exports from the country. Bangladesh's industry has been growing since the Multi-Fibre Arrangement (MFA) imposed quotas on some LDCs, but not Bangladesh. This meant that companies in Bangladesh, unlike those in China, could export as much as they produced. When the MFA quotas were lifted, China dominated but Bangladesh has continued to prosper despite this. Exports of clothing are now 16 per cent of the country's overall GDP (total value of goods and services), and the average income has almost doubled in the last 20 years. However, many garment workers do not earn enough to feed their families – it seems that some people are getting very rich, while others are staying poor. In 2011, 30% of the country's population lived below the poverty line.

Retailers	Sales (2007–2008)	Profits (2007–2008)	Country where retailed	Country where produced	Monthly wages of workers	'Living wage' – enough to feed family and provide shelter	Conditions of workers in six Bangladeshi factories that produce for the three retailers
Asda (Walmart UK)	£16.7 billion		UK (Gross National Income: US$2,608 billion)	Bangladesh (Gross National Income: US$75 billion)	1,663-2,900 Taka (approx £18–30)	5,333 Taka (approx £60)	• Long hours (up to 80 hours a week) • Breaking labour laws • Forced overtime
Tesco	£51.8 billion	£2.8 billion					• Unpaid overtime • Verbal abuse • Physical abuse • Sexual harassment and abuse
Primark	£1.9 billion	£233 million					• No right to form a trade union • No contract • No maternity leave or sick leave

This table shows data on UK retailers and Bangladeshi workers from a report by the campaign group War on Want.

Indian garment workers near Rajasthan do embroidery work for Anokhi, a company that is renowned for its good labour conditions and investment in workers and their community.

Fashion and the environment

All global industries have an environmental impact, but some impact more than others on humans and society. Below are some of the ways in which the growing global fashion industry is causing environmental problems, and impacting on human development.

SPOTLIGHT

Damaging processes

- Producing maximum cotton yields means using chemicals and water on the farmland.
- Energy used in the manufacturing process, including the manufacture of synthetic materials (mainly from oil), causes gases to be emitted into the atmosphere.
- Each garment has 'clothes miles' as it travels often several times around the world, and this causes carbon dioxide to be released into the atmosphere.
- High consumption means high waste as many unwanted products are thrown away.

Impact on the environment

- The gases emitted contribute to climate change.
- Factories contribute to global water shortages.
- Synthetic materials take a long time to dispose of and decompose.
- Habitats and wildlife are harmed by actions such as forest clearance and the use of fur in fashion.

Impact on people

- Growing cotton takes over cropland, creating food supply issues.
- Machinery has replaced some workers, causing job losses.
- The health and safety of workers is at risk, because of chemicals, fatigue, and other occupational hazards.

The race to the bottom

Large, powerful companies in the fashion industry compete with each other to deliver the best prices to their consumers. This results in a global race to find the cheapest sources of garments and materials, known as the 'race to the bottom'. Profit is a higher priority for many companies than checking that their garments and products are ethically produced, and there are many reports and news stories that demonstrate the poor working conditions and unfair pay in factories producing fashion items cheaply. For example, the campaign group War on Want produced the report *Fashion Victims* in 2005 and *Fashion Victims II* in 2007, highlighting the unfair working conditions and wages of workers producing clothes for Asda, Tesco and Primark. One problem is that companies do not invest in factories but contract to local companies instead. These companies are known as 'footloose multinationals'. Local contractors have to compete by offering the lowest price, and workers do not have many choices.

University students campaign for a living wage for workers producing clothing for the high street retailer Primark.

SPOTLIGHT

Sweatshops

Some workplaces in the fashion industry inflict poor conditions on workers. These include very long hours, very low wages, and a lack of rights for employees. Factories that ignore the law regarding employee rights, or are based in a country where there are few employment laws, are nicknamed 'sweatshops'. Organisations and charities campaign against sweatshops, by using media exposure. For example, a recent protest against Primark, organised by No Sweat, included five politicians, a celebrity, and the National Garment Workers Federation of Bangladesh. Campaigners criticised conditions and wages in factories where Primark clothes are made. Several TV programmes have also criticised large clothing retailers recently in Western countries.

> " *I can't feed my children three meals in a day with my earnings. This is my fate.* "
>
> Ifat, a Bangladeshi garment worker in the report
> *Fashion Victims II*

Fashion and identity

The reasons why we follow fashion are wide-ranging, and connected to our identities, or image, in society. There are 'rules' for what is acceptable for different people – for example, the 'normal' dress of a teenager is different to that of someone in their thirties, or their sixties. A person's ethnic and socio-economic background also influences what they are likely to wear. Fashions change depending on setting, too – for example, a person's work outfit and shoes are often different from their weekend clothes, but both could still be up-to-date, fashionable, and recently bought. Furthermore, clothing and accessories can represent our status, and in some cases even show whether we are married. Fashion can advertise political beliefs, favourite music, religion, or cultural pride based on the colour, style, fabric and slogans on a t-shirt, suit or shoes. Vibrant and colourful West African dress in global cities such as London, Sydney and New York stands out and perhaps shows the wearers' pride in their culture.

Women shop for fashion accessories in Rajasthan India. Traditional styles of clothing such as the sari are still highly popular in many parts of India, while Western styles are also catching on.

> *The pantsuit is [Hillary] Clinton's uniform… her wardrobe is a way of reminding voters that a woman can have as much bravado as the boy.*
>
> *The Washington Post*, 2007

Fashion freedoms

Unfortunately, people's fashion choices sometimes cause them to be treated negatively or unfairly. There are many cases where people are excluded because of what they wear. If someone cannot afford labelled clothing and trainers, this can lead to issues such as bullying and harassment, and even theft by the victim in order to 'fit in'. In several cases of violent attacks on young people, clothing or footwear has been one of the issues raised in police reports and at trial.

> *They don't have to be like everybody else, but there is a great comfort to fitting in, there's a great comfort to feeling part of a peer group, part of a community.*
>
> Sarah Jessica Parker, BITTEN Clothing Website, 2008

No two t-shirts are the same

Globalisation is a complex process and there are many different sides to the global fashion industry. This industry impacts on our lives and our environment. Each fashion item consumed has a different route and story behind its production. In the case studies that follow, some of these routes and stories are explored.

For some young people, 'gothic' fashion like this is a way to stand out from the crowd and get noticed.

High street fashion: designed for all

The Australian department store Myer showcases its Spring/Summer Collection in 2008. Industry sales are increased through fashion shows and advertising.

The term 'high street' usually refers to shops that are in the very centre of cities and towns, providing affordable clothing to the mainstream, or most people in society. These shops are easily accessible, and many of them have larger sections for female fashion, as sales in this sector are highest despite a steady rise in men's fashion in the last few years. High street stores and shopping centres are the traditional outlets for the fashion industry in MDCs, but supermarkets, out-of-town stores, and internet websites are catching up. Sales online have steadily increased over the last few years, but unlike retail areas, most products are bought between Monday and Thursday (weekends are the busiest times for high street shopping).

Seasonal styles

The fashion season has always been an important part of the industry. Traditionally, designers and retail stores changed their stock twice a year, for Spring/Summer and Autumn/Winter. Since shopping has become more popular, and production of clothes has become cheaper, customers can afford to buy many more items, so they go shopping more often, and the shops change their stock to appear new and exciting. Now fashion seasons are much shorter. This means that the whole production chain has to speed up, impacting on every person in that chain.

SPOTLIGHT

Fast fashion

The trend for disposable, fast fashion has changed the global fashion industry. Retailers like H&M from Sweden, Zara from Spain, and New Look, provide quickly made, ever-changing stock. Supermarkets, including Tesco and Asda-Walmart, also change fashion stock quickly. Items usually take six weeks from design to point of sale, and are generally worn two or three times before being discarded when the next 'season' or stock arrives. If a popular celebrity is seen wearing a designer outfit, fans can buy an affordable version within two months. This fast process means that factory workers may be forced to work overtime to meet the demand, because factories will lose work with the large companies if they do not deliver the products on time.

Chinese workers sew t-shirts at the Bo Tak garment factory in Dongguan city, southern China.

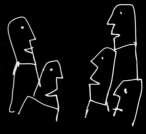

Information and fashion

Media and fashion have an interdependent relationship. Media advertising creates a demand for fashion items, as consumers often find out about products through TV adverts, magazines and other media products. For example, the films *The Devil wears Prada*, *Sex and the City* and *Confessions of a Shopaholic* all promote shopping. Media also raises our awareness. News companies occasionally publish stories about sweatshops and poor labour conditions in the industry. Sometimes this can help improve situations, as companies have to respond to these accusations, and investigate their own supply chain. However, they do not always know about every stage of the production chain, as it is complex and a pair of jeans that were made in Tunisia may have buttons from another country, which does not appear on the label. Some people argue that it suits TNCs to remain ignorant, because managers do not have to correct poor working conditions if they do not know about them.

In the film *The Devil Wears Prada*, Anne Hathaway plays a character working for a fashion magazine and trying to get to grips with the fashion industry.

Branding

Fashion companies develop brands carefully, through design, advertising campaigns, (often starring celebrities) and storefronts. Some fashion TNCs have several brands, each reaching a slightly different market. Examples of multi-branding are Gap, Banana Republic and Army & Navy in the USA, or Mosaic Fashions in the UK, whose brands include Oasis, Coast, Principles and Warehouse. Fashion items are products that people want, rather than need, so brands need to convince the customer that the fashion item will make them feel good.

Looking like a star

Feel-good fashion is often connected to celebrities, who are in advertising campaigns and often wear free clothes from a top designer as another form of advert. Many people wish they were rich, famous and beautiful, and copying celebrities' style is common. Asos.com, a major online retailer, capitalised on this, as it started out by selling props and outfits 'as seen on screen', so that people could get the celebrity look. Another brand of Mosaic Fashions, Anoushka, is described by the company as 'red-carpet glamour for everyday living'.

SPOTLIGHT

Credit and debt

As clothing companies become larger, transnational organisations, they have larger budgets and bigger bank balances. Some TNCs have diversified and also offer credit cards as part of the fashion industry. These cards are sold at the till by staff who usually get a commission or bonus, and they have a much higher interest rate than normal credit cards. The cards persuade the consumer to spend in that store, and generate more profit through the interest. Many retailers, such as Debenhams, are even offering credit cards, using their access to customers, in order to branch out into banking. Customers then accrue personal debt through shopping for clothes — not only by spending every week, but also through store and credit cards. The same company therefore makes money through sales and also through interest on the purchases.

The cotton t-shirt: a global journey

Cotton is the main material used to make clothing. Jeans, t-shirts and underwear are often 100 per cent cotton, while many garments contain cotton mixed with man-made fibres. Cotton fibre comes from the cotton plant, grown on large farms or plantations. Cultivating the crop can be back-breaking work. Slaves farmed cotton plantations on the American continent hundreds of years ago. More recently, cotton caused problems in Africa by occupying fertile land that farmers needed to grow food. Another issue today is the use of harmful pesticides in cotton-growing.

Cotton producers

Today, the world's major exporters of cotton are the USA, Australia, Uzbekistan, India and a group of 14 West African countries often called the Franc Zone. The US cotton industry is the largest in the world, located mostly in West Texas. It has grown stronger through new technologies and government support such as paying subsidies to cotton farmers to support their businesses. The US cotton industry has adapted to the global marketplace, and the subsidies paid help to keep it successful, but other countries cannot afford to pay or offer help to their farmers, which results in an unequal industry.

> *The rich countries continue their subsidies – that's a human rights issue... When I went to Mali and we went out into the fields, it was the women who were picking the cotton. They were poorer than they had been, three or four years before, because of the subsidies in the United States.*
>
> Mary Robinson, 2008, Ethical Globalisation Initiative, UN High Commissioner 1997–2002

Travelling the world

After cotton is harvested, it has to go through many processes before it becomes a t-shirt. For example, cotton grown in Texas may travel to China to be spun, knitted into fabric, and made into a t-shirt, and then shipped back to the USA to be sold in Florida. Alternatively, the cotton could be grown in Cameroon, shipped to India for production, then sold in the UK. China is the leading exporter of clothing, because it has a large population and a large amount of cheap and willing labour, so it is able to offer a good price.

Women's work

Many workers in the t-shirt manufacturing process are women, and child labour is also sometimes used. This is a serious concern, although the garment industry is often safer than other child labour situations across the world, where some children do heavy agricultural work or are even forced to fight in an army. Women in Chinese factories are vulnerable because many work away from their registered place of residence (*hukou*), which means that they could be breaking laws. In the 1950s everyone in China was given a *hukou* and was not allowed to leave that area, and although the laws have changed, some workers are unaware of their new rights and believe that factory managers could have them arrested. This makes them afraid to complain about poor conditions and desperate to obey their managers. Even so, many female workers in yarn factories and garment factories believe that the work is easier and more enjoyable than farming, their family industry. The fashion industry gives more freedom as hours are fixed and women can sit and talk as they work, although many state that it does not provide a living wage.

This world map shows the route of two different t-shirts from field to store. Many garment routes are more complex than this, incorporating many places along the way.

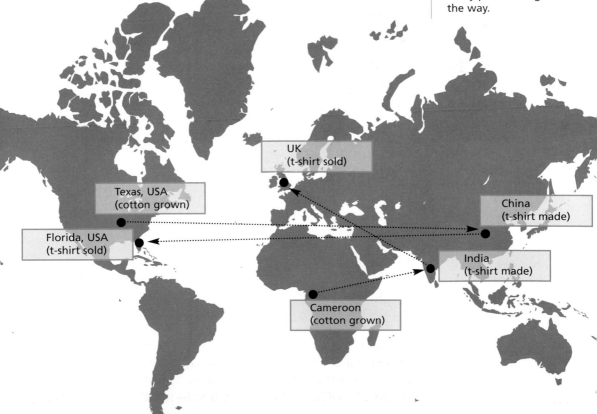

UK
(t-shirt sold)

Texas, USA
(cotton grown)

China
(t-shirt made)

Florida, USA
(t-shirt sold)

India
(t-shirt made)

Cameroon
(cotton grown)

After first use

If a new t-shirt isn't sold at first, it may be relocated to an outlet store or to T K Maxx, a specialist retailer in remaindered, returned and end-of-range products. After it has been bought and worn, it is often disposed of quickly. It may be given to a charity shop like the Salvation Army or Cancer Research, or it might be put in a textile-recycling bin. Companies such as LMB in London and Trans-Americas Trading Company in the USA separate used clothes for export. Some 'vintage' items are resold, or if the item is a good example of 'Americana', it might go to Japan. Clothes in poor condition are sold to rag-cutters to make rags for factories, and the poorest quality items are shredded into a fluffy material called "shoddy", to make insulation or even to be spun into a new t-shirt.

Threatened fashions

Cotton has been used in many different cultures around the world. In India and South Asia, the traditional sari and salwar kameez are most often made of cotton. Yukata and kimono robes in Japan, traditional African clothing, and the communist pyjamas of China are all popularly made from cotton. But as a country becomes richer, its fashions change too, and many men and women across the world are choosing to wear Western-style cotton clothes. The t-shirt is now worn so widely that it is threatening the survival of many traditional clothing designs. Fashions that closely link to culture, identity, religion or beliefs are being rejected in favour of those that symbolise power and money. Everyday Western fashion is considered a sign of wealth and success.

Waste and the environment

The production of cotton t-shirts has an impact on the environment. The global production process involves thousands of miles of travel, which uses energy and emits carbon dioxide, and between 2,000 and 7,000 litres of water are involved in making one t-shirt. Fertilisers and pesticides containing poisonous toxins are used in cotton cultivation, polluting the soil and causing deaths every year. The t-shirt may contain metal traces, formaldehyde and PCP (pentachlorophenol), which can be harmful to humans and to the environment. Farmers and factory workers are most at risk from these chemicals, as finished items of clothing contain only very low levels. However, some people choose to buy organic clothing to reduce the risk to themselves, their families, and farmers across the world.

Buying your t-shirt

Every time you buy a t-shirt, your life is connected to farmers, factory workers, transport workers who shipped it, and retail workers who sold it. This process might be different every time. You might be helping some people to achieve a better standard of living, and you might be supporting sweatshops and the prolonging of poverty without realising it. There are ways in which you can affect the global t-shirt industry. You have consumer power and can choose which companies to buy from, based on your knowledge. You can use the internet to find out which companies support sweatshops. You also have power as a citizen (and soon as a voter) to make sure you are happy with the laws about cotton trade in your country.

Apparel workers in Rajasthan, India, cut fabric pieces which will then be sewn at another work station.

CASE STUDY UNCOVERED

Sales in fashion accessories (including jewellery, handbags, belts and hats) increase yearly. In 2009, they accounted for more than £1 billion in the UK, and an annual value of US$30.7 billion in the USA. As in the garment industry, women's sales dominate, although men's accessory sales are growing and were valued at around US$6 billion in the USA in 2011. Women's handbags are the major seller, while jewellery and scarves are popular within men's sales.

Inexpensive items

The accessories industry has experienced the same race to the bottom (see page 16) as other sectors, and as a result people are able to consume more and spend less, because their products are made using cheap labour in LDCs. Although a financial downturn in 2008 affected the whole fashion industry, expert predictions that accessories sales would increase over the next few years were proved correct, as consumers bought new accessories to update old outfits.

These handbags for sale on the street in Hong Kong are cheap imitations of top designs. 'Fakes' like this are popular because they give the appearance of wealth without the expensive price tag.

SPOTLIGHT

Fast figures on the global accessories industry
- Sales increased by 37 per cent in the UK between 2003 and 2007.
- Handbags are the lead product in the industry in both the USA and the UK.
- Sales of men's accessories grew by 31 per cent in the USA between 2004 and 2008.
- The top high street retailers in the UK accessories market are Marks & Spencers, New Look, Claire's Accessories and Accessorize (2009).

Handbags

Between 2000 and 2005, UK consumers spent £350 million on handbags. Instead of buying one good handbag, as many women have done in the past, consumers today can buy several, in different styles and colours. Designer handbags, some costing several thousand pounds, are popular, and many women associate these handbags with status: a stylish handbag made by Gucci or Chloe is another way to look and feel as rich, beautiful and powerful as a celebrity. The trend for handbags is global, with fashionable women in Japan, Hong Kong, China and India, as well as Western women, carrying expensive bags. It is a sign of wealth across the world, although some feminists believe that shopping, and especially buying decorative handbags that serve as accessories rather than functional items, holds women back and labels them as frivolous and concerned with beauty over more serious issues.

> Women's resistance to the pressure to shop has been around for decades, and feminists have long believed that an ideal world would be one in which: *Women would stop focusing on what they wore or the size of their bodies, stop spending hours and hours at beauty parlours. As for shopping! Only a ninny [fool] pursued such an empty-headed activity – a deliberate male chauvinist conspiracy to distract women from serious matters.*
>
> The Independent, Ireland, 2007

Jewellery hazards

Jewellery sales also form a significant part of the accessories industry. However, many processes involved in jewellery production are dangerous, including gold, silver and diamond mining. There are dangers for people working with less precious materials as well. The process of making popular or 'costume' jewellery involves cutting, setting and polishing stones, sometimes in cottage industries or at home, but often in factories. Many workers suffer from silicosis, a disease affecting the lungs, caused by fine dust from cutting and polishing minerals and gemstones. There are more than 500,000 sufferers in China, according to the World Health Organisation (WHO).

Blood diamonds

Diamonds are considered the ultimate rich fashion accessory. They symbolise the wealth of the wearer, as well as emotional ties such as engagement and marriage. But the global industry of diamonds is not as elegant and sparkling as the end products. In Sierra Leone, diamonds mined and sold by rebels funded a civil war that killed thousands of people and caused many children to be taken as soldiers. The rough diamonds found in streams and in the soil were sold illegally to smugglers, or exchanged directly for guns.

Miners search for diamonds among the gravel at the bottom of a stream in Sierra Leone. Their industry has been safer and more controlled since 2003 (see Spotlight opposite).

> *In America, it's bling bling. But out here it's bling bang.*
>
> Leonardo Di Caprio in *Blood Diamond* (2006), set in Sierra Leone

> *Diamonds are associated with positive events in people's lives, any association with anything violent is something that has to be addressed by our industry and has been addressed and will be addressed.*
>
> Cecilia Gardner, World Diamond Council website, 2009

SPOTLIGHT

Governing trade

The Kimberley Process Certification Scheme is a legal process that has been in place since 2003 to control the movement of rough diamonds from mine to market. Some 74 countries worldwide have signed this agreement, stating that each stone must be accompanied by a certificate proving that it is not a conflict or 'blood' diamond. The official agreement acknowledges that it needs the help of companies and governments also, to regulate the diamond trade effectively.

Diamonds and HIV

Diamonds have always been a precious resource, and mining has always been a risky job, where workers are exposed to diseases such as malaria, silicosis and tuberculosis. Today, many people in diamond-mining areas in southern Africa have been infected with HIV, and there are frequent deaths from AIDS amongst miners. Mining areas are busy and over-populated, with temporary and migrant workers, especially men, who are away from their wives and families. This has led to a large sex industry in these regions, and men may have sex with HIV-infected prostitutes and carry the disease back to their families. Debswana, a large diamond company owned by De Beers and the government of Botswana, launched an HIV/AIDS programme in 2002. Employees and their families can attend education sessions given by their own community members, as well as receiving testing and treatment using antiretroviral drugs (ARVs), which are too expensive for many AIDS sufferers to afford otherwise. The programme of treatment has increased the productivity of Debswana workers and reduced the amount of deaths, making it so successful that workers in De Beers' gold and diamond mines in South Africa and Namibia have also begun to receive support and treatment. De Beers have said that HIV/AIDS management is not only part of the corporate social responsibility, but also plays a key role in the productivity of the company.

Many people spend a large amount of their wardrobe budget (and often money they don't have as well) on footwear, especially trainers. For example, Americans buy 2.4 billion pairs of shoes on average per year, which is almost eight pairs per person living in the USA. Nevertheless, the USA and European countries have mostly made a loss on the footwear industry over the last few years. This is largely because imports from the Far East, including China, Malaysia and India, always undercut prices. This has especially increased since 2005, when quotas on footwear imports were lifted. Although there are many criticisms of labour conditions in LDCs, consumers still prefer the cheapest price.

Workers finish shoes at a factory in the one of the four largest shoe-making districts in China. Close to half of the total number of shoes sold in the European Union are produced in China.

SPOTLIGHT

High heels and health

The global footwear industry's sale of very high heels for women has impacts on health, according to experts. Women suffer injuries such as strains, harm to joints and often get bruising, calluses or bunions. One organisation has estimated that the National Health Service in the UK spends £29 million a year treating foot injuries caused by high heels. However, the risks involved do not seem to deter most women from wearing high heels, and, like handbags, shoes are a product that women are generally prepared to spend more money on.

Cobblers and waste

In the past, shoes were expensive, hardwearing and difficult to find. Most people took their worn shoes to a cobbler to be repaired, rather than buy a new pair. Shoes were often black, to go with every outfit. Now they come in many different colours. Chinese and Vietnamese-produced shoes are cheaper on the whole, and we buy more, so the design of women's shoes reflects this, adding details that make shoes appropriate only in certain settings. This means that you 'need' more pairs. Waste is created when cheaply made shoes break, but also when high-quality shoes are thrown away because we stop liking them, rather than because of any flaw or damage. Most people in MDCs simply buy a replacement pair, though cobblers do exist and are popular in LDCs, where second-hand shoes imported from MDCs are fixed and sold.

Vegans and leather

Animal rights activists and vegetarians have created a demand for non-leather shoes. This growing market is largely made up of specialist shops and online companies selling quite plain footwear, although recently more stylish and fashionable shoes have been available for vegans and vegetarians. Natalie Portman, the actress who starred in three of the *Star Wars* films, has showcased a number of different vegan shoe designers, and for a short while promoted her own line of high fashion shoes with the design company Te Casan. Celebrity brands of fashion are very popular, as fans often buy the items that their favourite celebrity endorses, and recently many celebrities have actually designed the footwear and clothing items that they promote.

The actress Natalie Portman attends the launch of her celebrity vegan shoe line, 'Natalie Portman for Te Casan', in New York.

A man looks at trainers in the window of the Adidas flagship store in Beijing, China. Wearing trainers is increasingly a reflection of style and fashion, rather than simply a practical choice.

Trainer technology

In the last 20 years, the popularity of sports shoes has grown considerably. Trainers or sneakers are now worn not only for sport, but also with jeans and other outfits, in many different situations. The sports shoe has diversified and met this demand. Technological developments in sports footwear have not only included air pockets for bounce, and materials that allow exercising feet to 'breathe', but they have also included fashion features such as sewn patterns and large logos. Companies including Nike, Adidas and Reebok spend millions on marketing trainers for sports and fashion wear, and celebrity soccer stars such as David Beckham and Cristiano Ronaldo front huge advertising campaigns.

> *Logos have grown so dominant that they have transformed the clothing on which they appear into empty carriers for the brands they represent.*
>
> Naomi Klein, 2000

The anti-Nike campaign

Nike is one of the most popular global brands in the world. Children in some UK and US schools check their correct spellings not with a tick mark, but with a swoosh, Nike's logo. Owning Nike trainers is a dream of people all over the world. But Nike have received decades of criticism for poor factory conditions where their products are made, including accusations of child labour, pay below the cost of living, and intimidation of employees who want to form a union to protect their rights. According to the New Internationalist magazine, it would take only 4 per cent of Nike's marketing budget to pay every Indonesian worker a living wage.

Responding to bad press

Nike have responded in the last few years by becoming leaders in the Corporate Social Responsibility (CSR) business, which develops policies and monitoring systems for the well-being of employees and workers related to a company. News stories continue to emerge, but Nike's CSR team respond through comments and positive publicity. Because of their large profit margins, Nike can invest in unusual and creative programmes to improve human development and sustainable production. The Nike Reuse-A-Shoe project recycles any brand new or used trainers, making them into play surfaces for sport and children's parks.

Ethical shoes

Several shoe companies have developed production models that use more sustainable and fairer methods. For example, Blackspot shoes created a product called the 'Unswoosher', which is made of organic and recycled materials in a 'safe, comfortable union factory'. But this kind of organisation is sometimes criticised, because it takes the chance of development away from LDCs, and restricts trade to MDCs.

The American Football star Damon Allen endorses the Nike Reuse-A-Shoe campaign, which makes sports ground material out of recycled shoes. Nike often uses sports stars to promote its business.

PERSPECTIVES FOR DEBATE

"We can use the power of our brand, the energy and passion of our people, and the scale of our business to create meaningful change."

Nike website, Nike Responsibility section, 2009

"All empires must fall, Nike is no exception, it's the perfect time to rethink the whole system and demonstrate that small, indy brands have the power to steal business away from the megacorporations."

Blackspot by Adbusters, (Ethical Shoe Retailer), 2009

Alternative fashion: making a change

Alternative fashion comes in many forms, but usually it refers to the section of the industry that is smaller-scale, where companies use different business models and create more specialist products, to meet the specific demands of their customers. These demands might be about the kind of materials that are used, a more unusual style, or the social impacts of production.

Customer choice

Alternative fashion companies have flourished because of the support of their careful consumers. For example, the organisation Traidcraft has built much of its success on Christian church attenders who consider the moral issues of trade. Another reason that people choose these products is an interest in other cultures, as ethical and fair trade fashion uses styles from around the world. Looking different from the people around you is also important to some, and is another kind of fashion.

Niche market

The alternative fashion industry caters to niche markets, rather than the mainstream. The internet has helped alternative fashion companies, because their customer base is usually not large enough to open a shop in every city, but nationally they can generate enough sales via the web to succeed. Threadless, a t-shirt design company in the USA, and People Tree, the ethical clothing company most popular in the UK and Japan, have both flourished like this.

WEAR THIS SHIRT FOR 10 YEARS & SAVE 670 PIECES OF CLOTHING

Tom Kostigen, an author of 'eco' books, attends the Be Eco Chic fashion show in New York. Eco Chic and sustainable clothing are growing in popularity.

Consuming less

Many people are beginning to question the amount that is consumed through shopping, because of the environmental impact, and this has inspired new fashion opportunities. The famous three words: Reduce, Reuse, Recycle have found their way into the fashion industry, and have affected buying patterns. Some people choose to shop in charity shops, and reuse, adapt and customise existing items in their wardrobes rather than buy new clothing, accessories and shoes. Celebrities have endorsed this idea too.

Customising cool

The BBC Thread website encourages fashion fans to save money, be creative, make money, be sociable, and regain skills lost by modern communities, by customising their existing wardrobes, and also by going to clothes swaps, where people take their unwanted items and swap them for others. In this way, they achieve a new or vintage look that is still fashionable or cool but also ethical. Urban Outfitters, a global retailer, has the line Urban Renewal, where items are made from reused fabric. Top Shop held a whole week of environmental and social initiatives in June 2008 called Top Shop Wants Your Rubbish, which featured sustainable transport and gardening, as well as information about what Top Shop are doing to change the way they work. TRAID (Textile Recycling for Aid and International Development) is another organisation that is looking at textile recycling differently, as it uses fashion students to redesign and customise donated clothes for a more up-to-date look.

SPOTLIGHT

Ethiscoring

This table shows the 'ethiscore' of ten fashion retailers, according to the Ethical Consumer magazine's source, Corporate Critic. The score is based on how companies deal with a number of ethical issues in their operations, including: Environment, People, Animals, Politics and Product Sustainability. The higher the score, the more ethical the perceived approach.

Ethiscore	
American Apparel	14
People Tree	13.5
Urban Outfitters	9.5
Gap	9.5
Marks & Spencer	8
H&M	6.5
Top Shop	6
Primark	3.5
Tesco	0.5
Asda-Walmart	0.05

> *Fair trade? It's not good enough. It has to be organic fair trade. You've got 20,000 people dying every year of pesticide poisoning and you tell me that's not a social issue?*
>
> Katharine Hamnett – eco-pioneer,
> quoted in Eco-Chic, 2007

Pesticides and organic clothing

One movement within the alternative fashion industry is that of organic clothing, accessories and shoes. This requires knowledge of the whole supply chain, as the cotton or hemp must be grown organically, then continue to be processed without the use of chemicals such as finishers (these usually make products non-iron, wrinkle-free or stiffened). Agrocel is one such organic cotton producer in India, and the cotton is then processed locally in India and Bangladesh, before garments reach the markets.

Mahima ginning factory in Madhya Pradesh, India, processes fair trade and organic cotton.

Governing alternative trade

Fair trade in itself is becoming a sales feature, as it is more and more popular, but most consumers in this industry are keen to know where their money goes and to feel connected to the producers. This requires more governance and control than the rest of the fashion industry. There are several ethical certification schemes, including national fair trade brands such as Fairtrade UK, and an international organisation called IFAT – the World Fair Trade Organisation. However, criticisms of fair trade are also common, and a new scheme is being developed, called the Sustainable Fair Trade Management System (SFTMS). This certification and governing policy should mean that producers who want to show that every stage of their supply chain is both ethical and sustainable can do so.

SPOTLIGHT

Ethical school uniform

School uniform is now mass-produced for the cheapest possible price, which in the summer of 2011 was £8.50 from Marks and Spencers, £7 from Asda and £4.50 from Tesco. The school uniform pack includes a shirt, skirt or trousers, and a jumper or cardigan. But the same companies have been proven to use factories that pay their workers less than the minimum cost of living. Parents, schools and schoolchildren may be unaware that their uniform policy and standards are fuelling sweatshops and keeping the poorest countries poor. One organisation in the UK, called Clean Slate Clothing, began developing organic cotton school uniform free from pesticides that followed a fairer supply chain, to try to give parents the assurance that their children's uniforms did not involve sweatshops in their production.

> We have labour standards in our society. We have environmental standards in our society, but we let our companies go around the world to find the dirtiest and cheapest place to produce clothing to import back into our society, and we think that's fine. Children represent the hope of our society – we talk to them about ethics, but then we require them to wear school uniform that is produced like that.

Mark Rogers, founder of Clean Slate Clothing, 2008

Fair trade

Most fair trade organisations express the belief that trade should do more than make profit at any cost – it should also fight poverty, address inequality and help communities to develop. More than this, it should simply be fair, so that those involved get paid what they deserve for the work they have done, irrespective of what country they live in.

Beyond the smiling workers

Most of the information we receive about fair trade organisations is from those companies themselves. Websites, leaflets and even products show images of happy workers, making it difficult to be critical of such a movement. But many people still do debate the merits of fair trade fashion. Some common arguments are shown in the table opposite.

Workers knit gloves for the ethical retailer People Tree in Kathmandu, Nepal. The producer (KTS) provides education, training and jobs for underprivileged people in Nepal.

Arguments for fair trade	Arguments against fair trade
Fair trade not only allows workers to achieve basic standards of living, but certified fair trade organisations also pay a 'community premium' for the development of the local area.	Fair trade organisations create inequality as only those working for the company, living in a small surrounding area, can benefit, whereas whole areas of the world are in need.
Fair trade clothing and accessories are interesting, unique and beautiful products that often reconnect their wearers with natural materials.	Because fair trade companies are usually small, quality control and other corporate systems are less effective, so products have faults or are poorly designed.
Many fair trade products are handmade, which keeps alive precious traditional skills all over the world, important to the cultural heritage of those places.	Continuing to support processes where clothing is made by hand actually hinders development, as machine processes could make more money for those communities.
Fair trade is becoming so popular that even major fashion retailers are developing fair trade clothing lines – it is considered good business sense.	Fair trade as one consumer choice among many will not change anything, it is still consumerism at the end of the day – in order to affect real change you must examine the whole system of free trade, and use law and regulation to make trade fair. Also, the major retailers are competing with the small fair trade organisations, and winning, but their methods are not as ethical.

The future of trade

The community premium is a sum of money that each fair trade producer receives on top of the fair price, to invest in local community and infrastructure. This is the strongest reason to support fair trade for many, and consumers are creating positive change and development through their buying patterns. They are helping one small community, though, not more. Trade rules, a lack of proper regulation, and demand for cheap, fast fashion regardless of human cost are huge issues that can only be touched by alternative fashion TNCs. Overall, too many TNCs in the fashion industry are currently involved in exploiting people at a global level, and it would take more significant change, and more widespread support of ethical and sustainable traders and producers, to affect this.

PERSPECTIVES FOR DEBATE

"How can a few extra pennies a day from fair trade be celebrated as an outstanding achievement for the poor?"

Steve Daley, WORLDwrite, 2007

"Fair trade doesn't just mean paying a fair price. It is an entirely different way of doing business, where the objective is not profit at any cost, but to help people in the world's most marginalised communities escape poverty and promote sustainability."

People Tree, Fair Trade clothing retailer, 2009

Becoming an active global citizen

What is an active global citizen? It is someone who tries, in their own small way, to make the world a better place. To become an active global citizen, you will need to get involved in decisions that others make about your life and the lives of others around the world. Consider how the world could be changed, such as improving the environment, political or social conditions for others, and seek information about the issues from a wide variety of sources. Then go public by presenting your arguments to others, from friends and local groups to national politicians and global organisations.

In your life

It is easy to forget that we are all connected to the global fashion industry every day. Everything we wear has been made by a company to sell to consumers, either directly or indirectly. In order to engage with how fashion products are made, you could try the activities below.

1. Choose five items of clothing from your wardrobe, and see if you can find out what they are made from and where they come from.

2. Which is your favourite clothes shop? Visit it and have a look at the labels (or talk to the store manager) to find out from how many different countries the clothes are sourced.

3. Global trade is said to spread peace and cultural exchange across the world, as it helps people to work together instead of fighting or not communicating. The global fashion industry plays a vital role in this.
• Based on what you have read in this book, how much 'good' does the industry do? How could it do more?

4. Go to: http://www.direct.gov.uk/en/Environmentandgreenerliving/Greenerhomeandgarden/Greenershopping/DG_064424 and check out information about making greener choices when you shop for clothes.

• Do you have anything to add to this information, that you have learned about in this book?

5. Go to the Friends of the Earth's ethical fashion webpage: http://www.foe.co.uk/living/articles/ethical_fashion.htmland explore their tips for eco-fashion. Use the information to decide:
• How easy is it to avoid fast fashion?
• How does the webpage encourage you to think about the fashion industry?

6. Explore the world of second-hand clothes exporting at www.lmb.co.uk, a website produced by one exporting company. Work through the activities and information, and make sure that you find the link: 'Who gets my clothes?'
• Have you ever worn second-hand clothes?
• Why do you think that second-hand clothes may have gone out of fashion in your country?

Key terms for internet searches

Type these terms into a search engine on the internet and see what results you get. How many hits appear? Are the websites from around the world, and are there any information sources that surprise you?

- "race to the bottom"
- anti-Nike
- blood diamonds
- clothes miles
- clothing quotas
- corporate social responsibility
- cotton production
- cotton subsidies
- customising clothes
- ethical fashion
- export processing zones
- fair trade
- fashion quotas
- fashion season
- fast fashion
- free trade
- harmful pesticides
- multi-fibre arrangement
- sweatshop
- textile recycling

Data watch

Keep on top of global statistics by trying the activities below.

Visit http://www.worldmapper.org and click on the A to Z index of maps. Select and view maps 83 and 84, Clothing Exports and Clothing Imports.
- Who are the main producers and who are the main consumers in the global clothing industry?

On the CIA World Factbook website at https://www.cia.gov/library/publications/the-world-factbook/geos/xx.html' and look at Export Commodities in the Economy section.
- Using the 'Search' function on the top bar, see how many different countries export clothing, textiles, footwear and jewellery, by typing in the word, then pressing enter each time.

Consider the following data:

- 35 kg of clothing are bought per year by the average UK citizen
- £350 million are spent on handbags every year
- 2,000–7,000 litres of water are used to make a t-shirt
- 8 pairs of shoes are bought per person per year in the USA

Do a survey to find out your own fashion consumption rate, by estimating what your clothing consumption, and that of your friends and family, has been over the last month or year.
- How much did you buy, and how much was thrown away?
- Can you find out the weight of the consumption?
- Are you above or below average?

43

Topic web

Use this topic web to discover the themes and ideas in subjects that are related to the fashion industry.

Geography
Explore your family's cultural identity and diversity by asking what kind of clothes they prefer to buy and why. Consider what are the reasons – work, comfort, fashion, ethics, cultural rules?

Citizenship
Use a copy of a world map to create a spiderweb showing the connections that you have with other people around the world, based on where your clothes have come from. How many different countries do you connect with?

English
Design and write a magazine advert for a new fashion retailer that uses sustainable and ethical business practices. Make sure you tell customers about what they will get out of the fashion items, as well as how their items impact on people and the environment.

Maths
Find out roughly (cross-check your figures on several websites to get an estimate) how many pairs of shoes are bought each year in the UK, the USA and Australia. Then find population figures for those countries from https://www.cia.gov/library/publications/the-world-factbook and calculate how many pairs are bought per person in each country.

The Fashion Industry

Science
Find out about some of the different pesticides and chemicals that are commonly used in the garment industry. Make a table showing the pros and cons of using them.

ICT
Investigate three different online fashion websites and decide what is effective about them. What makes the websites easy to use? How do they use their sites to persuade you to buy items? Would they encourage you to shop online, rather than in a store?

History
Find out about the 'Make do and Mend' campaign from World War II. Why was it started? Would it work now?

Glossary

antiretroviral drugs A type of medication used to treat infections by retroviruses, most commonly HIV.

apparel Clothing or dress.

brand A symbol, mark or quality that characterises a product. It has been called 'a product's personality'.

climate change Significant changes in the world's climate, including temperature and weather patterns. Some people believe this is linked to human activity such as carbon emissions into the atmosphere.

consumption The purchasing of goods and services for use. In the fashion industry, this is measured by how many fashion items are bought and discarded by each customer.

endorse To show support or approval for a product.

exploitation Using human labour for the benefit of a company or organisation without giving fair return such as wages, decent working conditions and benefits.

feminist Someone who believes in the equality of women and men in both public and private life, such as careers, human rights and in the home.

formaldehyde A chemical compound that is used in many industries, and can be toxic, or even cause cancer.

haute couture (high fashion) Clothing or footwear made by exclusive top designers, and often custom-fitted for rich, private customers.

infrastructure The systems that support a country such as roads, water supply, waste, power supply, access to shops, and other resources.

interdependent When organisations, industries or individuals are mutually dependent on each other to make something work.

investor Someone who puts money into a project, business or industry, often in order to gain financial returns.

less developed countries (LDCs) Countries that have a lower income and poorer standards in health, nutrition, education and industry than more developed countries (MDCs).

mass-produce To manufacture goods on a large scale, often using factory assembly lines.

media exposure Publicity and presence in the media, often making something common knowledge or advertising a product or company.

migrate To move from one country or region to settle in another.

more developed countries (MDCs) Countries that have a higher income and better standards in health, nutrition, education and industry than less developed countries (LDCs).

niche Describing a focused, small section of an industry, such as the vegan shoe market, or the gothic fashion market.

organic Describing materials that come from living matter (animal or vegetable) and usually do not contain manmade or chemical products.

pesticides Chemicals used in agriculture to prevent crops being affected by insect or weed pests.

poverty line The minimum income needed to maintain a basic standard of living.

quota A limit or maximum quantity of a product. In the global fashion industry, quotas restrict the amount of apparel or footwear that can be imported or exported.

socio-economic Describes the financial and social situation of a person or group.

source To obtain products from other countries or businesses, for resale or use. Fashion buyers source goods for retail stores.

subsidies Payments made to an industry by its government.

supply chain The processes through which a product flows when being made, sourced and sold, involving a number of individuals and organisations.

sustainable Able to be maintained at a steady level for a long time, without causing environmental or social damage.

tariff A tax paid on goods when they are imported.

transnational company (TNC) A company that operates across several nations.

union An organisation of employees, formed to negotiate with their employer about pay, conditions and benefits.

urbanisation The process whereby people migrate to towns and cities, leading to more urban environments with increased traffic, shopping and leisure facilities.

World Trade Organisation (WTO) An organisation that deals with global rules of trade.

Index

Global Industries Uncovered

Contents of titles in the series:

WAYLAND